Success Tweets

For Speakers And Information Marketers

140 Bits of Common Sense Career Advice
All in 140 Characters or Less

BUD BILANICH
The Common Sense Guy

DAVE VANHOOSE

DUSTIN MATHEWS

Front Row Press
191 University Boulevard, #414 • Denver, CO 80206 • 303.393.0446

This book is dedicated to those brave souls who willingly share their knowledge, wisdom and expertise in order to help other live their dreams.

Introduction

This is a success book in 140 tweets. It's a real book that will help you create the speaking and information marketing success you deserve.

It gives you 140 pieces of common sense speaking and info marketing success advice, all in 140 characters or less.

It will tell you how to succeed as a speaker and info marketer, 1 tweet at a time. You'll get the essentials with no fluff.

Creating your speaking and info marketing success should be fun and exciting. This book will show you how to do it.

Your time is valuable. You don't want to waste it. That's why you get 140 pieces of advice twitter style, in 140 characters or less.

Building a successful speaking and info marketing career is simple common sense. It's not hard, but you need to do it right.

Focus on the 8 Keys to speaking and information marketing success.

Clarify the purpose and direction for your life and career.

- Create clarity by figuring out what success means to you personally.
- Create clarity by creating a vivid mental image of yourself as a success.
- Create clarity by determining your personal values.

Commit to your speaking and info marketing success.

- Take personal responsibility.
- Take personal responsibility by setting and achieving high goals.

- Take personal responsibility by choosing to react positively to the people and events in your life; especially the negative ones.

Build unshakeable self confidence.

- Build your confidence by choosing to be optimistic.
- Build your confidence by facing your fears and acting.
- Build your confidence by surrounding yourself with positive people.
- Build your confidence by finding a mentor to help you create your success.

Get Competent.

- Become a lifelong learner.
- Get fit.
- Manage your time life and stress well.

- Learn what it takes to become a speaking and info marketing success.

Create Positive Personal Impact.

- Create positive personal impact by creating and nurturing your unique personal brand.
- Create positive personal impact by being impeccable in your presentation of self; in person and on line.
- Create positive personal impact by knowing the following the basic rules of business etiquette.

Become a Dynamic Communicator.

- Become a dynamic communicator by demonstrating strong conversation skills.
- Become a dynamic communicator by writing clearly and succinctly.

- Become a dynamic communicator by mastering public speaking skills.

Build Strong Relationships.

- Build relationships through self awareness. Use this knowledge to better understand others.

- Build relationships by paying it forward; give with no expectation of return.

- Build relationships by using conflict to strengthen, not weaken, relationships with the important people in your life.

Take Care of Yourself

- Do what you need to feel good about yourself, your life and your career.

The tweets that follow will show you how to put these 8 Keys to work — and create the speaking and info marketing success you deserve.

Will tweet books replace traditional books? Probably not. But this book will get you started as a speaking and info marketing success.

Enjoy this book. But remember, we want to talk with you, not to you. Please tweet what you think about our ideas. @BudBilanich, @DaveVanHoose1, @DustinMathews.

Each of the points we've made above is less than 140 characters.

See? You can communicate a lot of useful information in 140 characters or less. Enjoy the following 140 tweets.

Clarity

CLARITY

1

Define exactly what speaking and information marketing success mean to you. It's easier to hit a clear, unambiguous target.

CLARITY

2

The more clear you are about what success means to you personally, the easier it will be to create the life you want.

CLARITY

3

Think of your purpose as your personal mission; why you are on this earth. Your direction is your vision for the next 3 to 5 years.

CLARITY

4

The mightier your purpose, the more likely you are to succeed. It will give you a strong foundation when the winds of change shift.

CLARITY

5

Your vision should be a BHAG; a Big Hairy Audacious Goal. Make it something that is really worth working for and accomplishing.

CLARITY

6

Make sure you really want to be a speaker and info marketer. Work you love will make it easier to create the success you deserve.

CLARITY

7

Don't focus just on making money. If you do, you'll be asking too little of yourself. Focus on being useful in this world.

CLARITY

8

Happiness doesn't come from getting more things. It comes from finding a worthy purpose and pursuing it.

CLARITY

9

Emerson says, "Good luck is another name for tenacity of purpose." Pursue your purpose as a speaker and info marketer tenaciously.

CLARITY

10

Create a vivid mental image of your success. This vivid image will keep you motivated and moving forward when things get tough.

CLARITY

11

Think of your vivid mental image as a blueprint. It is a plan for success, but you still have to do the work to make it a reality.

CLARITY

12

Visualize the euphoria of success, not the pain of failure.

CLARITY

13

Use affirmations to create your success. Affirmations are statements about the future stated in the present tense.

CLARITY

14

Clarify your personal values. They are your anchor and your guide to decision making in ambiguous situations.

CLARITY

15

Your values come from deep inside you. Spend the time necessary to discover them. Hold fast to them; honor them by your actions.

Commitment

COMMITMENT

16

You're in charge! Commit to taking personal responsibility for creating the successful speaking and info marketing career you deserve.

COMMITMENT

17

Take personal responsibility for your success. No one will do it for you. Remember: "If it's to be, it's up to me."

COMMITMENT

18

Aim high. Set and achieve high goals —
month after month and year after year
after year. Do whatever it takes to achieve
those goals.

COMMITMENT

19

Make your goals S.M.A.R.T. : **S**pecific, **M**easureable, **A**chievable, **R**elevant and **T**ime Bound.

COMMITMENT

20

Focus on your goals several times a day. Spend your valuable time only the things that will help you achieve them.

COMMITMENT

21

List the reasons for each goal you set for yourself. These reasons will come in handy you when you get tired and frustrated.

COMMITMENT

22

Create goals in all areas of your life: career, personal, business, family, hobbies, health and fitness. Make sure they are congruent.

COMMITMENT

23

Plan how you will achieve your speaking and info marketing goals. Do whatever you have to do, not feel like doing, to achieve them.

COMMITMENT

24

Stuff will happen as you create your speaking and info marketing success. Choose to respond positively to the negative stuff.

COMMITMENT

25

Failures are the tuition you pay for success. When you have a setback, choose to react positively and learn something.

COMMITMENT

26

Persistent people keep going; especially in the face of difficulties. Keep at it; you will reach your speaking and info marketing goals.

COMMITMENT

27

Don't be afraid to fail. You fail only if you don't learn something from the experience. Treat every failure as an opportunity to grow.

COMMITMENT

28

It's not what happens to you, but how you react to it. Don't dwell on the negative, use it as a springboard to action and creativity.

COMMITMENT

29

Don't let a slow day get you down. If you come back empty handed in your quest for success, get up the next day and keep working.

COMMITMENT

30

Vision without action is a daydream. No matter how big your plans and dreams, they'll never become a reality until you act on them.

Confidence

CONFIDENCE

31

Focus on what you are becoming — a speaking and info marketing success. This makes it easier to believe in yourself.

CONFIDENCE

32

Choose optimism. It builds your confidence. Believe that today will be better than yesterday and that tomorrow will be better yet.

CONFIDENCE

33

Optimism is contagious. Become a positive, optimistic person. Surround yourself with positive people. They will build your confidence.

34

Everyone is afraid sometime. Self confident people face their fears and act. Look your fears in the eye and do something.

CONFIDENCE

35

Defeat fear. Here are 4 steps to deal with fears that can sabotage your success. Identify it. Admit it. Accept it. Do something about it.

CONFIDENCE

36

Procrastination is the physical manifestation of fear and is a confidence killer. Act — especially when you're afraid.

CONFIDENCE

37

Surround yourself with positive people.
Hold them close. They will give you
energy and help you create the success
you want and deserve.

CONFIDENCE

38

Jettison the negative people in your life. They are energy black holes. They will suck you dry; but only if you let them.

CONFIDENCE

39

Find a mentor. Mentors are positive people who will help you find the lessons in your problems and failures and to use them to move forward.

CONFIDENCE

40

Identify the self confident people you know. Pay attention to how they act and carry themselves. Watch what they do. Act like them.

CONFIDENCE

41

Fake it till you make it. Act as if you expect to be accepted, and you will be. This will boost your self confidence!

CONFIDENCE

42

Self confidence comes from within. Outside reinforcement and strokes can help, but you have to build your own confidence.

CONFIDENCE

43

Be as enthusiastic about the success of others as you are about your own. Help all the people around recognize that they are special.

CONFIDENCE

44

Give so much time to building your self confidence and improving yourself that you have no time to criticize others.

CONFIDENCE

45

Take stock of yourself. What are your strengths? What are your weaknesses? Confident people emphasize their strengths.

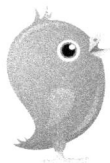

Competence

COMPETENCE

46

Become a lifelong learner. The half-life of knowledge is rapidly diminishing. Staying in the same place is the same as going backwards.

COMPETENCE

47

Learn as fast, or faster, than the world changes. In a world that never stops changing, you can never stop learning and growing.

COMPETENCE

48

Stay focused. Don't get distracted. Treat time as the precious commodity that it is. Manage your time and life well.

COMPETENCE

49

Break large projects into smaller chunks. They are not so overwhelming that way. Set mini milestones for yourself.

COMPETENCE

50

Get organized. Organize your time, life and workspace. Sweat the small stuff. Success is in execution. Execution is in the details.

COMPETENCE

51

The better you feel, the better you'll perform. Live a healthy lifestyle. Eat well. Exercise regularly. Get regular checkups.

COMPETENCE

52

Determine your peak energy times. Schedule "high brain" tasks then and "low brain" tasks at times when your energy is lowest.

COMPETENCE

53

Don't take yourself too seriously. Lighten up. It will help you master yourself and become an outstanding performer.

COMPETENCE

54

Get into a high performance mindset. Don't question yourself. Trust your skills and abilities. Do what you know how to do.

COMPETENCE

55

Good truly is the enemy of great. Don't settle for good performance. Today, good is mediocre. Become a great performer.

COMPETENCE

56

All successful speakers and information marketers have a killer presentation to use from the platform and in webinars.

COMPETENCE

57

There are 5 keys to a presentation that sells: Introduction, Story, Offer, Body and Close. Here's how to use all of them successfully.

COMPETENCE

INTRODUCTION

58

Gain instant credibility by being introduced by an influential leader or have an introduction video do it for you.

COMPETENCE

INTRODUCTION

59

Grab the audience's attention early. Put them at ease. Start your presentation with some appropriate humor.

COMPETENCE

INTRODUCTION

60

Get your audience into a "Yes" state. Do this by asking questions to which they are likely to only respond "Yes."

COMPETENCE

INTRODUCTION

61

Give your audience inside access. Tell them exactly what you are going to be telling them, and exactly what you are going to do.

COMPETENCE

INTRODUCTION

62

Be credible; separate yourself from everyone else by sharing your past accomplishments.

COMPETENCE

INTRODUCTION

63

Frame your offer in the introduction and make promises. Remember, it is better to under promise and over deliver.

COMPETENCE

STORY

64

Facts tell, but your story sells. Your story gives your audience a chance to connect with you on a more personal level.

COMPETENCE

STORY

65

Tell your story in a way that the audience gets a feel for you as a human being. Make them aware of your successes.

COMPETENCE

STORY

66

Every story has a turning point. This is the pivotal moment which explains why and how you chose success and empowerment.

COMPETENCE

STORY

67

Show your audience how your life changed after you implemented the ideas you are going to teach them.

COMPETENCE

STORY

68

Share your success lifestyle. Let the audience know that by taking action, they too can live the same way.

COMPETENCE

OFFER

69

Target the problem you will help the audience solve. Turn up their pain before you offer your solution to their problem.

COMPETENCE

OFFER

70

Create a Unique Selling Point (USP), to separate you from the competition. Explain it to the audience.

COMPETENCE

OFFER

71

If there are similar products to what you offer, so show why your product is THE solution.

COMPETENCE

OFFER

72

Tune into WIIFM (What's In It For Me). Make sure you let the audience knows exactly what is in it for them.

COMPETENCE

OFFER

73

Most people don't like to have to work very hard, make an offer that is easy to use, or better yet, done for them.

COMPETENCE

OFFER

74

Show both the features and benefits of your product. A home based business is a feature. The freedom to work from anywhere in the world is a benefit.

COMPETENCE

OFFER

75

Strengthen your close by anticipating potential objections the audience may have and providing solutions to them.

COMPETENCE

BODY

76

Use photos to show the benefits of your offer, and what it can do for your prospects.

COMPETENCE

BODY

77

Show your faith in the audience. Tell them you believe they can have the success and lifestyle you're selling.

COMPETENCE

BODY

78

Provide social proof of the value of your offer. Get testimonials from satisfied customers, pair them with photos. Audiences like faces.

COMPETENCE

BODY

79

Make sure your sign up is easy to use.
The easier it is to use, the easier it will be
to convert.

COMPETENCE

CLOSE

80

Show the audience a complete picture of what they are getting during your close.

COMPETENCE

CLOSE

81

Build up massive value during the close. List every individual part of your complete system and what the audience would pay at retail.

COMPETENCE

CLOSE

82

Establish a special one-time discount.
Inspire the audience to take action
immediately. Reward the action takers.

COMPETENCE

CLOSE

83

Create scarcity in your call to action. Limit the number of discounts. This will encourage the audience to ACT NOW.

COMPETENCE

CLOSE

84

Just about everyone has been ripped off in the past, so always offer a personal money back guarantee. It's good practice.

COMPETENCE

CLOSE

85

Give it all away for free! This can be done through affiliate programs, or through referrals. Refund the price of your offer when prospect meets criteria.

Positive Personal Impact

POSITIVE PERSONAL IMPACT

86

Create and nurture your unique personal brand. Stand, and be known for, something. Make sure that everything you do is on brand.

SUCCESS TWEETS FOR SPEAKERS AND INFORMATION MARKETERS

87

Your personal brand should be unique to you, but built on integrity. Integrity is doing the right thing even when no one's looking.

POSITIVE PERSONAL IMPACT

88

Build your personal brand. Do whatever it takes to make sure that people will think of and remember you in the way you want them to.

POSITIVE PERSONAL IMPACT

89

Nurture your network. What your friends, colleagues, clients, and customers say about you is how others will think of your brand.

POSITIVE PERSONAL IMPACT

90

Demonstrate respect for yourself and others in your dress. People will notice and respond positively to you.

POSITIVE PERSONAL IMPACT

91

Be well groomed and appropriate for every situation. Always dress one level up from what is expected. You'll stand out from the crowd.

POSITIVE PERSONAL IMPACT

92

"Business" is the first and most important word in "business casual". Dress like you're going to work, not a sporting event or club.

POSITIVE PERSONAL IMPACT

93

21st Century technology has created new etiquette rules. Learn and use them to appear polished when you're on line.

POSITIVE PERSONAL IMPACT

94

Be gracious. Know and follow the basic rules of etiquette. Everybody likes to be around polite and mannerly people.

POSITIVE PERSONAL IMPACT

95

When someone compliments you, just say "thank you." When someone criticizes you, say "thank you, I'll work on that".

POSITIVE PERSONAL IMPACT

96

Learn and use simple table manners. Good manners make you look polished and poised and help you concentrate on the conversation.

POSITIVE PERSONAL IMPACT

97

Always act like a lady or gentleman. It's not old fashioned; it's smart business and leads to a successful life and career.

POSITIVE PERSONAL IMPACT

98

Keep your breath fresh. Brush after meals and coffee. Use the strips. Don't chew gum. Ever. It makes you look like a cow.

POSITIVE PERSONAL IMPACT

99

Say "thank you" often. You'll succeed in your life and career, build a strong personal brand and leave a legacy of being a nice person.

POSITIVE PERSONAL IMPACT

100

Be courteous. It costs you nothing, and it can mean everything to someone else. It also helps in getting what you want.

Dynamic Communication

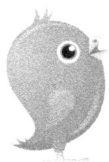

DYNAMIC COMMUNICATION

101

All dynamic communicators have mastered three basic communication skills: conversation, writing and presenting.

DYNAMIC COMMUNICATION

102

Speak from your heart. Show that you care — about yourself and the people with whom you are speaking.

DYNAMIC COMMUNICATION

103

A brief conversation with the right person can greatly help — or hinder your speaking and info marketing success.

DYNAMIC COMMUNICATION

104

Conversation tips: be warm, pleasant and gracious and sensitive to the interpersonal needs and anxieties of others.

DYNAMIC COMMUNICATION

105

Demonstrate your understanding of others' points of view. Listen well and ask questions if you don't understand.

DYNAMIC COMMUNICATION

106

Become an excellent conversationalist by listening more than speaking. Pay attention to what other people say; respond appropriately.

DYNAMIC COMMUNICATION

107

Live people take precedence over phone calls. So continue in person, face to face conversations, rather than answering your cell phone.

DYNAMIC COMMUNICATION

108

Use the 2/3 - 1/3 rule. Listen two thirds of the time; speak one third of the time. Focus your complete attention on the other person.

DYNAMIC COMMUNICATION

109

Remember and use people's names. Look for common ground with the people you meet. Find out about them, their hobbies and passions.

DYNAMIC COMMUNICATION

110

Become a clear, concise writer. Make your writing easy to read and easy to understand. Use simple straightforward language.

DYNAMIC COMMUNICATION

111

Write clearly and simply: short words and sentences; first person; active voice. Be precise in your choice of words.

DYNAMIC COMMUNICATION

112

Become an excellent presenter. Script your talk. Practice until you are perfect.

DYNAMIC COMMUNICATION

113

Presentation steps: 1) Determine the message. 2) Analyze the audience. 3) Organize the information. 4) Design visuals. 5) Practice.

DYNAMIC COMMUNICATION

114

Presentations are easy to create. Write your closing first, your opening next. Then fill in the content. Practice, practice, practice.

DYNAMIC COMMUNICATION

115

Discipline yourself to prepare for presentations. Practice out loud until you are totally in sync with what you're going to say.

Relationship Building

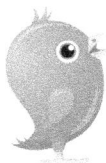

RELATIONSHIP BUILDING

116

Get genuinely interested in others. Help bring out the best in everyone you know. Others will gravitate to you.

RELATIONSHIP BUILDING

117

Use every social interaction to build and strengthen relationships. Strong relationships are your ticket to success.

RELATIONSHIP BUILDING

118

Everyone has something to offer. Never dismiss anyone out of hand. Take the initiative. Actively build relationships with others.

RELATIONSHIP BUILDING

119

Get to know yourself. Use your self knowledge to better understand others and build mutually beneficial relationships with them.

RELATIONSHIP BUILDING

120

Pay it forward. Build relationships by giving with no expectation of return. Give of yourself and time to build strong relationships.

RELATIONSHIP BUILDING

121

When meeting someone new ask yourself, "What can I do to help this person?" By thinking this first, you'll build stronger relationships.

RELATIONSHIP BUILDING

122

There is no quid pro quo in effective relationships. Do for others without being asked or waiting for them to do for you.

RELATIONSHIP BUILDING

123

Be generous. By giving with no expectation of return, you'll be surprised by how much comes back to you in the long run.

RELATIONSHIP BUILDING

124

Be happy to see others succeed. Use the success of others to motivate yourself to greater success.

RELATIONSHIP BUILDING

125

Trust is the glue that holds relationships together. The more you demonstrate trust in others, the more they will trust you.

RELATIONSHIP BUILDING

126

Resolve conflict positively. Treat conflict as an opportunity to strengthen, not destroy, the relationships you've worked hard to build.

RELATIONSHIP BUILDING

127

Be a consensus builder. Focus on where you agree with other people. It will be easier to resolve differences and create agreement.

RELATIONSHIP BUILDING

128

Be responsible for yourself. No one can "make you angry". Choose to act in a civil, forthright, constructive manner in tense situations.

RELATIONSHIP BUILDING

129

We all make mistakes. Own up to yours. You'll become known as a straight shooter — honest with yourself and with others.

RELATIONSHIP BUILDING

130

Become widely trusted. Deliver on what you say you'll do. If you can't meet a commitment, let the other person know right away.

Take Care
Of Yourself

TAKE CARE OF YOURSELF

131

Be kind to yourself. Accept yourself. Love yourself and who you are.

TAKE CARE OF YOURSELF

132

Take care of yourself. Do what you need to do to feel good about yourself, your life and your work.

TAKE CARE OF YOURSELF

133

Choose to be you — don't wait for other people's permission to live your life and pursue your speaking and info marketing success.

TAKE CARE OF YOURSELF

134

Be hopeful and abundant. Hope defeats fear. Abundance defeats scarcity.

TAKE CARE OF YOURSELF

135

You get what you expect. Expect the best as a speaker and info marketer and you'll get it.

TAKE CARE OF YOURSELF

136

When you focus on what's going right in your life, things will begin going right more often.

TAKE CARE OF YOURSELF

137

Blame, resentments and envy get in the way of taking care of yourself and creating the success you deserve.

TAKE CARE OF YOURSELF

138

Forgiveness precedes peace and harmony. Forgive others. More important, forgive yourself.

TAKE CARE OF YOURSELF

139

Every morning when you wake up, envision yourself as having a great day, filled with success and happiness.

TAKE CARE OF YOURSELF

140

Every night before you go to sleep, think about the good things that happened to you that day. Sleep in appreciation of them.

ONE MORE THING

141

And, because we always over deliver, here is one more very important tweet…

Knowing is not enough. Successful speakers and info marketers will act on this advice. Take action. Become the success we know you can be.

About The Authors

@BudBilanich, a life and career success coach helping you create the success you deserve. Let me help you succeed. www.BudBilanich.com

@DaveVanhoose1, master speaker trainer helping you close more from the stage or web no matter what your niche. www.DaveVanhoose.com

@DustinMathews, expert marketing strategist helping you get more eyes on your products and more prospects in seats. www.DustinMathews.com

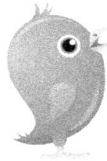

Success Tweets for Speakers and Information Marketing makes a great gift!

Quantity discounts are available from the publisher.

Call 303.393.0446 to inquire about quantity pricing.

Claim Your Personal Wealth & Freedom Strategy Session
(Valued at $250)

---

www.SpeakingEmpire.com/strategy-session

Congratulations! You're only seconds away from gaining more wealth and more freedom. To schedule your strategy simply go to the address below...

www.SpeakingEmpire.com/strategy-session

On this webpage that we've setup just for you, you'll be welcomed by a special video that will share with you how to take your speaking to the next level.

---

www.SpeakingEmpire.com/strategy-session

---

www.ingramcontent.com/pod-product-compliance
Lightning Source LLC
LaVergne TN
LVHW051519080426
835509LV00017B/2107